Ink and Reveries

Cristal Gonzalez

BookLeaf
Publishing

India | USA | UK

Presentation by *BookLeaf Publishing*

Web: www.bookleafpub.com

E-mail: info@bookleafpub.com

ISBN: 9789360946494

First edition 2024

For my son, Theo ...

Make your dreams happen,

my love.

For my dad, who always

knew I would be a writer.

For the Universe,

Who inspires me.

ACKNOWLEDGEMENT

First and foremost, I would like to acknowledge my dad, who always believed in my love of words. Twenty years have gone by since I lost him, but he is with me everyday, encouraging me to pursue my talents and dreams. My mother, who may not be as specific in her encouragement, but who has always reminded me that I can do anything I put my mind to. She is the one who helps me when I am my own worst enemy and I don't think I have ever been able to properly thank her for pushing me to be better. I've seen her go through the worst possible moments: losing a husband, losing her parents. Everytime, she has shown me how to survive the worst with grace and determination.

To my son, I hope this book shows you that you can always achieve your dreams. You have been my inspiration to be a better person, to be happy, and to set the best example for you as you explore the world around you. You are the light in a world full of doubt, and my motivation to show you anything is possible. To Leo, thank you for filling my life with furry chaos and love, paws and puppy kisses. You always have tried to keep my life full of light even when darkness threatened to drown me. You will always have a special place in my heart.

Every high and low in my life has filled me with inspiration, so I have to thank the Universe for sending me the experiences that have shaped me. And lastly, to the one who gave me the courage to do this: thank you.

PREFACE

There is a childhood picture of me, where I am about 4 or 5 years old. I am sitting at a little table with a toy typewriter in front of me. I am completely enthralled with whatever it is I think I am writing. There is a pure joy on my face — the joy you see on other kids' faces when they are riding a bike or playing baseball.

I think my affair with words began before I could speak. I have always loved how words have the power to do so much. They can build you up; they can tear you down; they can inspire greatness; they can evoke emotions lost to time. The most fascinating thing about words is that they only have the power we give them. Think about how many people hate the word "moist". It is a simple adjective that describes a state of being. Yet some people can't stand it.

I never considered myself a poet. I always felt I had so much to say and a few lines or metaphors and euphemisms could not possibly encompass it all. One day, I realized something: Words have power. I needed to find a way to make that power mine. Poetry provided that. It began with the precision of finding the exact right word to say what I needed to. I began to consider which words evoked the feeling that I needed to explore. That I wanted my reader to feel and explore as well. That is what drew me in and I was hooked. The constant search for the perfect way to express myself so my reader could feel it, somehow, in their own way, like I did.

Illumination

Sometimes I dream in colors
Bold and vivid
Clear and bright.
My mind blurs the
edges
and softens the sharp lines
as I dance through a
riot of colors and clouds.

Other nights, when my mind
can't be still,
the world becomes
sepia toned —
like the whole world is illuminated
By candlelight.
My body entwined
with yours;
sensation is all I know.

Then there are nights
With no color at all.
Sharp and bright,
but never truly clear.
The world becomes a
void
where I slowly disappear.

Scattered Pieces

It is an exquisite and exhilarating pain
that touches my soul just so,
as I gather the scattered pieces of
Hope and Heartbreak with the
simple words, what if?

Like the Universe, it's warmth
expands within me day by day,
along with the elegant pain of
letting go.

And all the while, just like sand,
acceptance trickles through my
scarred hands.

Treasure Box

There is a box
that lives on my dresser.
A simple wooden box,
delicately carved and treasured.
Itself an exquisite memory —
"A love undone..."

Open it up and
the past becomes present:
A watch, delicate and feminine;
A love letter full of
forgotten plans and hopes;
A spur of the moment drawing
made with love for me.

It is the photographs that
are the true
time machines.
The evident happiness in
my past self shown and seen
only reminds me how
it has faded from my face
and dreams.

A Moment

Coincidence
Fate.
The universe's plans
The impossibility of how
Our life takes shape
The sheer improbability of
The moments in our lives
That created who we are
From stardust and a thought.
Is control just an illusion
Of our primal, evolving minds
As we stumble through existence
Chaos in disguise.

I see my father's smile.
The universe in my son's eyes.
The sunrise on the mountains.
The promise in a smile.
The impossibility of existence
Creates miracles in
My eyes.

The Unease of Complacency

Am I a cloud?
No substance, feeling —
Fleeting.
Melting as I go.
As if I have no
       No Heavy Heart;
or maybe I'm the single
beam of light
from a far star away.
Always twinkling
in the night
As if to say,
I'm OK.
Yet every star is blinded
       within the light of day.
The sun rises every morning,
       and Suddenly
It's not OK.

Sunrise. Sunset.

Between sunrise and sunset.
Missing what was and
longing for what's to come:
a melody.

Memories play tribute
Imploring and seducing
A moment in time.
An instant becomes retaliation:
an accusation.

Mistakes of long past loves and
mourning for the souls
abandoned in the midst
of swirling snow
haunt the deepest memories.

Now in the still desert night
the singing of crickets surround
us with the laughter of those who
Loved like us.
Between sunrise and sunset.

Handle with Care

There is a place
inside my mind
where I go to wonder and
Daydream.
Where the impossible
becomes possible —
Dreams become realities.
For a moment,
Time stands still.

There is a place
inside my heart
where I learned to carry
light and dark and
every shade between.
Where I carry a candle lit
for desires that burn
deep within.
Desires that would be
quenched harshly in
the realities of life.

There is a place
inside my soul
where fragile hopes and dreams

can thrive.
So everyday we can wake up
and have something more to give.
Sustaining ourselves
with what we can,
even if it's not real.

But in our hearts and minds
and souls,
there they always live.

Moonlight Serenade

Big band music playing in the background of
a clear night amidst the reality of life.
Words that cannot be taken back
on one end and
words that did not want to be heard
on the other.
They watched Orion and a shooting star;
it was a moment in time where he could be what
he wanted
and she could be herself.
She let herself
go soft and
let him see who she really was
before the wall around her heart
went up to keep people out.
He showed her he wasn't what the world
believed;
there was a heart there, too.
He was honest and let himself sink into
their shared fantasy world of that night
when nothing else mattered but
Being.
The impossibility of their situation and
the bittersweet nostalgia of missed chances,
a future of stolen moments

and eventual goodbye…

But for one night
The desert sand was their
Dance floor
Their stage
Their reality —
For a moment.

Ember

There is profound—
there is all-encompassing—
then there is plunging—
      Deep into
      Your soul.
It changes who you were
      and who you are to be.
Never will you be the same.

      To love,
I gave Myself.
I was consumed.
I wandered.

Love became abstract
      A role to fulfill,
      Nothing more.
Yet in the quiet moments
      In my Soul,
The fire burned.
And it burns still.

Migrant

Their feet are tired.
It is hard to say what is worse —
the brutal heat that sucks
the moisture from your very being
or the bone-breaking cold that
seems to permeate every desert
they stop in.

Their little legs can only take so much.
There is desperation to do this;
to risk death to avoid almost certain death.
Escaping where a place where Life and Death
are not concepts
but realities.
There has to be something better than that.

The river is stronger than they thought and
their little legs can only do so much;
she could only do so much.
At least they found a better place. Their dream
came true: something better.

"Give me your moneyed, your whiteness,
your sparse immigrating numbers yearning for
Fame.

The wretched trash of your society;
send these, your useless, your money
seeking golddiggers.
Yet turn away the brown tired face
of those who only wish for
something better."

Stories of Spirits

The house is quiet.
What have these walls seen?
What remnants of spirits
linger
In these corners and seams?

Do those thoughts and spirits
linger
because this is where they
dream
of the love and happiness
They felt within these walls?
Or do they stay because they
can't break free of
the bonds they felt
shackled them here?

And so I sit
within these walls
that have seen and heard
so much.
Wondering if my story
will be happiness
or not.

La Llorona

Beset by voices in the
Night,
She wanders.
Always alone.

The hands were
Rough.
A man who worked
The fields
Real men work with
Their hands.
Those hands soothed
  His son's brow,
So similar to his own.
They lovingly brushed
His daughter's soft hair.
Those hands that once caressed
  Her.
No more.

The mists float off of the water,
  Thick that time of year.
At night, the Moon hid
  The mournful eyes
That watch us in

the Night.

Her neck, the stem.
Her head, the flower.
Rough hands squeezed
        The stem.
Harder, while
The children lay in
        Gentle sleep.
Mama is cast adrift,
        Alone.
Parted from her fragile life.
Her children, all the while,
dreaming of
        Laughing in the light.
They call her La Llorona,
Stealer of innocents;
        But she was not the thief
        That stole a life
        On that misty night.

So she cries
        Alone at night.
They say he watches,
        Hands clasped tight.
Always wandering the mist,
        Always blamed for doing
        What someone else had done.

Some say that if you walk at night,
Her sobs will beckon and
Beseech you
to listen while
        The mists shroud all but
        Her
        Sad mournful eyes.
Those eyes that
Watch us in
        the Night.

Monsters in Plain Sight

Dreams are what
      demons are — they
Smile in that
handsome face. That's
where lies the danger
of a Cloud-Nine - loving
Fate.
To float above
To live a lie
It's all the truth
They say.
The Devil smiling
      In his way
Shadows dancing on
      His Handsome face.

Absolution

Always the pull of
Fate
dragging us
Here and There.
And in the end, you may
find out, that you're
really Nowhere.
How do you find
a way out
When you've moved
both Here and There?
You sometimes may be
        Somewhere
Yet it still feels like
        Nowhere.
So we stand still, in
        fear of finding yet
        another Nowhere.
But what can one find
Standing still?
Perhaps our new
Somewhere.

Abyss

Darkness fills the crowded
air. The Deadly
Friendly
Air.
Grasping with a dying
breath —
       the safe, the friendly
       Air.
What once was safe,
What once was ours
Beyond now our control.
And those who peer
unafraid into the dark —
       those souls are
       the first to go.
What will they say when
We are dead
       Left rotting in our
       graves?
That it's ok to breathe
       that safe,
       that Friendly,
Deadly
       Air.

Fairytales

In fairy tales my grandma told
there were always princesses and
dragons —
fairies and Prince Charmings.

In her stories, though,
there was a twist:
Prince Charming was a
bonus and
her Dragon helped her
Fly.

The princess was never
helpless;
she stood her ground
and fought.
She saved herself,
when others could not.

There was a moment
I forgot
the strength she passed to me.
So I fight to find it,
because she's part of me;
always her princess
in disguise.

Darla

Twilight
Gradually comes on.
The sounds of a mockingbird and
Children enjoying the lasts
Vestiges of
Sunlight.

An old dog
Playing the puppy
In her eyes I see
She is tired.
She has given us her life
Her love
Her care
Her absolute trust
That we would love her
Care for her
In her youth
In her adulthood
In her old age.

A brindle coat shines
In the sun
Legs that once throbbed
In pain

No longer hurt
They are straight
Strong.

For a moment
I see her in her prime:
Majestic
Free
So happy she trips over her own feet.

Twilight
Has arrived.
The mockingbird is silent.
The stars have begun to come out.
An old dog enjoys her days
Content to leave
With the sun.

A Simple Day

It is quiet in the morning
as I lay wide awake in bed.
Your breaths are sweet and even,
as the sky brightens the day.

I gaze into your sleeping face
and see my own face is there.
Your hands are your father's in miniature,
yet no longer tiny like before.

As you dream, I wonder about
the kind of man you'll be.
Your eyes slowly flutter open;
I see the possibilities within.

Seeing the world through your eyes
is a privilege and so true.
Everything is an adventure.
Everything is new.

As the day wakes up and up we go;
we explore the world anew.
That is why a day with you
is never simply just a day.

The Magic of a Quiet Snowfall

I have always loved an almost dreary type of
weather.
Desert thunderstorms that leave a riot of color
in their wake;
Snowstorms that make me want to sink deeper
into
my warm bed;
Lazy afternoon rain clouds that help me relax
as they play their own unique melody.

But a quiet nighttime snowfall is a
unique experience of magic.
It is a quiet and precious stillness
as these battered little ice particles
fight their way down to the ground.
Majestic and violent;
the only movement in the serenity
of the night.

I breathe in the icy cold air as if
my body needs to take in the
perfect stillness of that
one perfect moment.
Time becomes dependent on the

delicately falling snowflakes.
They float, slowly and surely,
making time stand still.

Nature is quiet because nothing can
disrupt the magic of this
perfect, peaceful moment.
The trees are tranquil as they are coated
with their elegant dressings of silver and white;
the streetlights lost their garish glare and cast an
ethereal glow. The world is calm in the midst of
this still and silent symphony.

As the world softens,
I soften with it, because in those
impossibly still moments
anything and everything is possible.
The colors of the sunrise begin to
lighten the world: the stark contrast of the
snow against the darkness fades to gray,
to sepia, to light.
The snowflakes still gracefully
dance through the air, but
time resumes as the magic fades.

What I Could Never Be

Caught in the ether between
existing and not being real.
Frozen in a moment;
I captivated you.
I enthralled you.

You wanted what you imagined;
something broken to build up.
Something rare for only you,
a special kind of love;
with dreams and hope, you
treasured me deep within your heart.

If we could will what
was never there into life,
I would have been exactly that.
The girl you built up in your
thoughts and dreams; and
our life would be your
dream within a dream.

But what you fell in love with,
I could never be.
I was caught in the ether
between existing and a dream.

Wonderland

Falling down the rabbit
hole
Sideways up and
upside down.
I've always loved
the story
of a girl that
can't be found.
To live in imagination;
Behind the veil —
what lies?
Chasing the white rabbit
dreams can sort of come true.

The smile in the moonlight
the sudden change of
mood.
We are all the Mad Hatter
and all of his guests too.
A tiny, shiny little bat;
a rabbit that's seen better days
and a girl who
looks with Wonder,
but truly never wakes.

We all have our lost
Wonderland
when we have let
our fear
and pain
paint the Roses Red.